Reading & Writing

The Age of the Book

Reading & Writing

The Age of the Book

Marshall Cavendish
Benchmark
New York

This edition first published in 2009 in North America by Marshall Cavendish Benchmark.

Marshall Cavendish Benchmark
99 White Plains Road
Tarrytown, NY 10591
www.marshallcavendish.us

Copyright © 2003 Italian edition, Andrea Dué s.r.l., Florence, Italy

Library of Congress Cataloging-in-Publication Data

Rossi, Renzo, 1940–
The age of the book / by Renzo Rossi.
    p. cm. — (Reading and writing)
  ISBN 978-0-7614-4321-6
  1. Books—History—Juvenile literature. 2. Writing—History—Juvenile literature. 3. Printing—
History—Origin and antecedents—Juvenile literature. 4. Paleography—Juvenile literature.
5. Scriptoria—Juvenile literature. I. Title.
  Z4.Z9R67 2009
  002.09–dc22
                              2008032310

Text: Renzo Rossi
Editing: Cristiana Leoni
Translation: Erika Pauli
Design and layout: Luigi Ieracitano
Illustrations: Alessandro Baldanzi, Leonello Calvetti, Lorenzo Cecchi, Azzurra Giacomelli,
Sauro Giampaia, Luigi Ieracitano, Studio Stalio

Photographs: Scala Archives p. 6

Printed in Malaysia
1 3 5 6 4 2

Contents

Books for the Few

Today, books are commonly used by and available to everyone. You can find books in many places, including the bookstore, the library, and the newsstand. But it hasn't always been this way.

Once upon a time, books were expensive and most people didn't have a need for them. Indeed, very few people knew how to read. In the Middle Ages monks wrote books by hand, patiently copying the Bible as well as the works of ancient authors. In Late antiquity, Saint Jerome translated the Bible into Latin. His translation, known as the Vulgate, served as a model for all the later versions in various languages.

Opposite: Bishop Ulfilas converted Goths to Christia Since the Goths h no written langua; he invented the Gothic alphabet a translated the Bibl into the Germanic language.

Below: This minia shows Saint Jeron distributing copies the Vulgate.

Among the Slavic Peoples

The Slavic peoples, like the Goths, did not know how to write. At then end of the 9th century, in order to spread Christianity among these peoples, two Greek missionary saints, brothers Cyril and Methodius, invented an alphabet containing 40 characters. Cyril and Methodius translated the sacred scriptures into the Slavic language.

The Cyrillic alphabet, used today in Russia, the Ukraine, Serbia, and Bulgaria, is derived from this first Greek-Slavic alphabet. It was expanded by Saint Clement, a disciple of Cyril and Methodius.

Opposite, top: The Cyrillic alphabet.

Below: This illustration from a medieval book depicts Cyril and Methodius composing the first Slavic alphabet.

СОВЕТСКАЯ

А З БУК А

Right: Ancient Slavic script, called glagolitic, which was used in old religious texts.

Parchment

The fragile papyrus sheets that had been used for writing for centuries in Europe were eventually replaced with vellum, or parchment, which was more costly but much more durable. Parchment is made from the treated skins of calves, goats, lambs, and sheep. It was invented in the 3rd century BCE in Pergamum (in present-day Turkey), a city that was large and rich and that had an imposing library.

Washed with water and lime, the hides were scraped on the outside to remove the hair. Then, while still wet, they were stretched on a wooden frame and left to dry in the sun. Scraped again till they were smooth and thin, the skins were then whitened with chalk and smoothed with pumice. The parchment sheets were cut into regular leaves, folded in half, and bound to make a book (codex).

Below, left: The t
ner scrapes the h
stretched on the
frame with a spec
crescent-shaped
knife.

Below, right: The
Codex Amiantinu
an 8th-century Bi
composed of 1,0?
parchment leaves
folded in half for
total of 2,060 pag
20 x 13 inches
(51 x 33 cm) in si
Weighing almost
75 pounds (34 kg
it required 1,500
calf skins.

Artisans make parchment in their workshop.

11

Irish Monasteries

In the 7th century CE, Irish monks who copied texts developed a tiny, orderly, and harmonious script with clear, round letters.

Illustrated codices of extraordinary beauty were created in these monasteries, which were important centers of European culture. The monks made copies not only of sacred texts, but also of works on literature, history, and law. With their intricate interlacing artwork, the designs that decorate these books reflect the art of the Celts, the ancient inhabitants of Ireland.

Left: Intricate art work, such as thi initial from the Gospel of John, decorates the *Du Codex.*

Opposite: A lion, symbol of Saint Mark, decorates a page in the *Willi Gospel.* Willibror was a preacher in late 7th century.

Below: A typical monastery

belltowe

cemetery

guesthouse

chur

porter's house

farmhouses

13

The Writing of Charlemagne

In the 9th century, few laypeople knew how to read or write. Even the emperor Charlemagne, the most powerful man in Western Europe, could neither read nor write correctly, nor could the members of his court.

Nonetheless, Charlemagne understood how important education was and founded many schools at his cathedrals. He also worked to enrich the monasteries where the monks skillfully copied the religious and secular texts of antiquity using a new, clearer script called Carolingian minuscule. This type of writing was simple and soon replaced the Roman uncial script.

AAAAAA a

Above: The Carolingian minuscule, ancestor of our printed characters, evolved over time as capital letters were gradually transformed into lower case.

Opposite: The monogram, or seal, of Charlemagne was formed from the letters of his Latin name— Karolus Magnus.

Above: The sale of a piece of land is witnessed by a notary. Outside the monasteries, writing was used mainly for contracts and administrative documents.

For the Glory of God

In the Middle Ages Europe was filled with monasteries, many of which had great libraries, known as *scriptoria*, where the monks patiently copied the sacred scriptures in beautiful writing. It was a way, in addition to prayer, to give glory to God.

In a time of misery and widespread violence, the regularity and consistency of the script mirrored the serenity and dignity of monastic life. The pages were often decorated with beautiful letters at the beginning of each paragraph and with illustrations called miniatures (they were drawn with *minium*, a red pigment), as well as with gilding and other bright colors.

Below, left: The l[e]
Q is adorned wit[h]
knight fighting a
dragon in a medi[eval]
manuscript.

Below, right: Mo[nks]
devoted to writin[g]
were called *aman[u-]*
enses because the[y]
wrote by hand
(*a manu* in Latin[)]
They used quill p
and ink.

VID

MIRV

16

ying manuscripts
very tiring work.
monks' backs
d and their
ight was strained.
y often had to use
es (like the pair on top),
h were invented at the
of the 13th century.

In the Shadow of the Cathedrals

With the Carolingian minuscule, the scribe monks had a clear, elegant script that was eventually adopted throughout the Christian West.

Cathedrals in the new Gothic style sprang up across Europe and the writing style was modified. Both indicated that the Western world was ready for change, and more and more people were learning to write. The elongated and angular shape of the new Gothic script echoed the forms of the new cathedrals, which featured forests of spires and soaring heights. In Gothic writing the decorative effect prevails, making it harder to read.

In 15th-century Florence, where the rediscovery of classic Greek and Roman cultures revived the arts, the scholars of the time, known as humanists, used a softer and more rounded script that was actually a slightly modified return to the Carolingian minuscule. It was used to transcribe the works of the great authors of antiquity.

Left, background: pointed silhouette a Gothic cathedra

Below: A lower-ca *m* and *r* in Gothi script.

chants had to
w how to write
to manage their
nesses. In the
century, the
y created
ersities finally

gave them a
chance to learn to
read and write.
Up until then, only
clerics, monks,
and court scribes
were literate.

The Paper Revolution

Paper, the most universal medium for writing, was invented in China at the beginning of the 2nd century, when papyrus and parchment were still being used in the West.

It was the Arabs in Spain and Sicily who introduced this new material to Europe. In the 13th century, important paper-producing establishments were already active in many towns, and the ragman became a familiar figure as he passed from house to house, collecting old clothing, cotton, and linen rags to be used to make paper.

Paper would later be made with cellulose fibers, obtained from the trunks of trees, particularly pines. This is how we still make paper today.

Right: Ragmen sold their linen and cotton directly to the paper factories.

Opposite, botto The paper facto in Fabriano wa of the most pre gious in Europe It opened durin the 12th centur

Left: To make high-quality paper the Chinese soaked linen fiber in large tubs of water and lime until it was reduced to a pulp. A layer of pulp was then raised with a densely woven sieve. After being dried in the sun, it became a sheet of paper.

Printing at Last

In 1449 a German silversmith named Johannes Gutenberg invented movable type. He cast approximately a hundred copies of the letters of the alphabet in metal, and applied them to wooden blocks. With these characters, Gutenberg composed, page by page, the text of an entire volume of the Bible.

Above: The Gutenberg family coat of arms.

Using a press similar to the ones already in use to squeeze grapes, he pressed the inked type, or matrix, on a sheet of paper. The result was a perfectly legible printed sheet that could be reproduced many times.

This method saved an enormous amount of time and money. Before Gutenberg's invention it took the monks months, or even years, to produce a single copy of a book. Printing with movable type opened the way to the easy production and distribution of books.

Left: Every movable character was cast backward, like a mirror image, so that the characters, once inked and pressed on paper, were printed facing the right way.

The print shops in [Gut]enberg's time [emp]loyed several [wor]kers (*above*). [Gut]enberg sometimes [deco]rated the [first] letter on a [page] with a small [face] called a grotesque ([inset]).

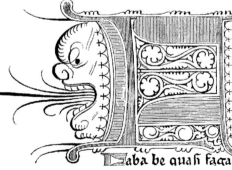

in latinis dicconibus po
mus utifama filius. In c
ds ūo dcōnibus ph. ut
pheus pheron. Doc tam
scire debemus. ꝙ non ta
fixis labijs ꝓnucianda
quō ph. atꝙ B solū inter
sicut dicit priscianus in
mo libro majoris.
Faba be quasi faca. a facin quod ē comede

But the Chinese Were First

Gutenberg's movable type was not really a new invention, because the Chinese had been printing with movable, reusable characters since the 11th century.

Before that they were already printing woodcuts. The calligraphers traced the characters of a text on a thin sheet of paper that was glued facedown on a block of wood or on a seal. The wood or stone around the characters was cut away by carvers so that one would have a text in relief: the matrix. To print it, all one had to do was ink the matrix and press it on a sheet of paper.

Opposite: Workers cut and ink the wooden matrix in Chinese print shop

Below, left: A stone matrix was used to print the pages in t book.

Below, right: Red i was applied to a se with incised letters make this impressi

25

Characters and Printers

Gutenberg had used the Gothic style letters, which resembled hand-written letters, as models for his characters. In this way, he was able to compete with the professional book-copyists.

Barely twenty years later, however, calligraphy was no longer fashionable and printers began to design new characters that were more varied, more legible, and more modern. The aesthetic reasons were flanked by practical reasons, since the printing technique was developing rapidly.

Below: Florentine mathematician L Pacioli proposed letter system base on geometric con struction in 1509.

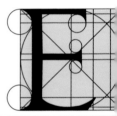

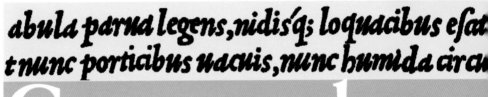

Above: Characters designed by Claude Garamond (e 16th century) and English typographer William Caxt (c. 1480) are still used today.

Left: A pad for inking the type.

26

Left: The first publishing trade-mark to appear in a printed book was that of German publishers Johann Fust and Peter Schöffer in 1475.

...osite, center: Famous
...tian printer Aldus
...utius designed a set of
...acters in the early 16th
...ury. The font was named
...ne, after its creator.

...t: Printing
...es in the 16th
...ury were manu-
...operated.

A Book for All

In Germany, after Gutenberg's invention, there was one book that was printed and made available more than any other: the Bible, which had been translated into German by the monk Martin Luther.

Luther had defied the authority of the Church of Rome, which he thought was corrupt. He maintained that everyone was free to read the holy scriptures. This is why he translated the Bible into German. Prior to his translation, the Bible was only available in Latin, a language only priests could read. People depended on priests to explain the text to them. Luther wanted everyone to be able to read and interpret the scriptures for himself or herself.

Above:
The frontispiece is the first edition of Luther's translation of the Bible.

He translated both the New Testament and the Old Testament, enabling the Protestants, the followers of his doctrine, to read them.

Eventually, births, deaths, and weddings were written down in the family Bibles, which passed from one generation to the next.

A peddler of popular books and almanacs
shows his wares to interested buyers.
As printing spread, he became a familiar
figure in towns and villages.

Index

Page numbers in **boldface** are illustrations, tables, and charts.